Praying the Word

From Psalms 119

By

L. O. Ovbije

ISBN: 978-1-944411-10-7
Copyright © 2023 by Rev. L O. Ovbije
Ovbije World Outreach Ministries, Inc.
P.O. Box 966
Clarkston, GA 30021-0966
U. S. A.
Website: owom.org
Email: theword@owom.org

Published by SOIL Foundation, Inc.
P.O. Box 966
Clarkston, GA 30021-0966
U. S. A.

All scriptures are from King James Version (KJV)
Printed in the United States of America.

DEDICATION

To God the Father, who love the world he
created and sent into the world Jesus
Christ his only begotten Son, To Jesus
Christ who came into this world in the
flesh, died, buried and rose from the dead
triumphantly to redeem every human
being God created and God made in his
own image and likeness, this Jesus Christ
of Nazareth has made redemption
available for any human being that will
trust and believe in him. And to the Holy
Spirit, who continuously reveal Jesus
Christ to individuals and people daily.
I thank God for my dear father who
taught me discipline and my precious
mother who taught me grace and
forgiveness. Both taught me
unconditional love. Both love me
unconditionally.
Pray in the language you speak daily. Do
not pray to impress people or God. There
is no language on earth that is superior to
your language. Pray in your own
language. Pray in the language you
understand, God wants to hear from you
now.

I Timothy 3:16

ACKNOWLEDGMENTS

To my wonderful parents: Chief J. E. Ovbije & Mrs. Margaret O. Ovbije, and to my siblings. My father was a man that lived a life that left an excellent and lasting impression on me. My father and mother taught me unconditional love; my mother taught me grace and forgiveness. Our family knew the meaning of a loving, secure and rich home because of my father's presence. I thank God for the private elementary school at Sapele: Children Nursery School, where I attended. It was there that I encounter God for the first time in prayer in a very early age.

To my precious pastor and his lovely wife, both were strong examples of a man and a woman devoted to God. I was fortunate to have pastor & Mrs. Umukoro, both disciples me. I thank them both for their daily early Morning Prayer life. To the men of God who also impacted my prayer life, W. F. Kumuyi and Benjamin Udi.

Finally to my sweet, precious, wonderful wife: Theresa Spearman Ovbije, a woman of God, whom I simply call "sweetie".

PREFACE

Praying the Word From Psalms 119. The book of Psalms is in the Old Testament of the Bible. It is part of the Old Covenant of the Bible. A covenant is a divine Agreement made by God Almighty with an individual, a group of people or his entire creature and creation. Most Covenants are sealed with blood. In the Bible there are various Covenants God made with individual and with people. Most of the various Covenants are found in the Old Testament. This book is not about Covenants. However, it is very important that you know when praying, not if you pray, but when praying, that you know what covenant God has with you. The Covenant that God has with you governors your prayers. The Covenant that God has with you is a New Covenant seal with the blood of Jesus Christ. Jesus Christ alone is the mediator of this Covenant. Therefore, you do not have any other mediator. Jesus Christ is your only mediator; He is your only acceptable Sacrifice to God for your relationship with God. No other sacrifice can take the place of Jesus Christ. You can only establish a relationship with God by and through Jesus Christ alone. Anything and anyone else is religion. Beware of religion, it can be an outlet for the plans of the devil, and most time it is. Religious leaders and Politicians are the very agents that crucified Jesus Christ. Therefore, when praying from Psalms 119, you should pray in the revelation of the New Testament, which is the New Covenant sealed with the blood of Jesus Christ. In Psalms 119, you will see these words often; Judgments, Precepts, Righteousness, Law, Ways, Covenant, Statutes, Testimonies, Truth, Commandments, Thy Word: these are the WORD of GOD. Psalms 119 focus on the vitality and the importance of the WORD of GOD. The Old Testament is a shadow of things to come. "But he answered and said, It is written, Man shall not live by bread alone, but by every word that proceedeth out of the mouth of God."

St. Matthew 4:4

"And to Jesus the mediator of the new covenant, and to the blood of sprinkling, that speaketh better things than that of Abel."

Hebrews 12:24.

1 **Blessed are the undefiled in the way, who walk in the law of the** LORD.

2 **Blessed are they that keep his testimonies, and that seek him with the whole heart.**

3 **They also do no iniquity: they walk in his ways.**

__Boldly Say:__ Father in the name of Jesus, I thank you that I am a doer of your word and I do not deceive myself. Father I thank you that I do live by your word. Father I thank you that I do keep your word. Father I thank you that I do seek you daily with my whole heart. Father I thank you that do not plan to sin, but if I sin I will repent immediately and I will boldly apply the precious blood of Jesus Christ to myself with my mouth. Father I thank you that I do not practice sin, in Jesus name, Amen.

4 Thou hast commanded us to keep thy precepts diligently.

5 O that my ways were directed to keep thy statutes!

6 Then shall I not be ashamed, when I have respect unto all thy commandments.

Boldly Say: Father in the name of Jesus, I thank you for teaching me your word by your Holy Spirit which dwells in me. Father I thank you that you commanded me to keep your word because you love me, Father I thank you that you did not suggest to me to keep your word, but because you love me, you commanded me to keep your word. Father I pray that my ways will be directed by your word. Father I thank you that I am not ashamed of your word. Father I thank you that I have hid your word in my heart that I may not sin against thee. Father I thank you that your word is a lamp unto my feet and a light unto my path. I do esteem thy word above my necessary food. Father I thank you that your word is sweeter than honey to my taste. Father your word will I forever hungry for, never to be satisfy, to apprehended he that has apprehended me, in Jesus name, Amen.

⁷ I will praise thee with uprightness of heart, when I shall have learned thy righteous judgments.

⁸ I will keep thy statutes: O forsake me not utterly.

⁹ Wherewithal shall a young man cleanse his way? by taking heed thereto according to thy word.

Boldly Say: Father in the name of Jesus, I thank you that I will praise you with uprightness of heart, for I have study your word and your word is pure. Father I thank you that I do hide your word in my heart, Father I thank you that I am a doer of your word. Father I thank you that your word does give me direction and your word does keep me from sin. Father I thank you that I am cleanse by your word. Father I thank you that your word is a lamp unto my feet and a light unto my path, in Jesus name, Amen.

¹⁰ With my whole heart have I sought thee: O let me not wander from thy commandments.

¹¹ Thy word have I hid in mine heart, that I might not sin against thee.

¹² Blessed art thou, O LORD: teach me thy statutes.

Boldly Say: Father in the name of Jesus, I thank you for your precious word. Father I pray that I will always seek your face. I pray that I will always hungry for your word. Father I pray that I will always put your word above things. Father I pray that I will never compromise your word. Father I thank you that your word is righteous and pure, in your word I do take refuge. Father I thank you that your word is always in my heart and before me. Father I thank you that your word have I hid in mine heart, that I might not sin against thee. O Father, teach me your word, in Jesus name, Amen.

¹³ With my lips have I declared all the judgments of thy mouth.

¹⁴ I have rejoiced in the way of thy testimonies, as much as in all riches.

¹⁵ I will meditate in thy precepts, and have respect unto thy ways.

Boldly Say: Father in the name of Jesus, I thank you that your word is for the now. Father I thank you that your word never change because you never change. Father I thank you that I do live by your word, for man cannot live by bread alone but by ever word that proceed out of your mouth. Father I thank you that I do declare your word daily with my mouth. Father I thank you that I do cherish your word above riches. Father I thank you that your word is the meditation of my heart all day. I rejoice at your word, for the way of your word is my way, in Jesus name, Amen.

¹⁶ I will delight myself in thy statutes: I will not forget thy word.

¹⁷ Deal bountifully with thy servant, that I may live, and keep thy word.

¹⁸ Open thou mine eyes, that I may behold wondrous things out of thy law.

Boldly Say: Father in the name of Jesus, I thank you that I will delight myself in your word. Father I thank you that I will not forget your word, for your word is always before me. Father I pray that I will always give your word the right of way in my life daily. Father I pray that I will never take vacation or holiday from your word. Father I pray that your favour will always encamp around me, that sinners may know that you are my very own Father and I am your very own child. Father I pray that you will open my eyes, that I may behold wondrous things in your word, in Jesus name, Amen.

¹⁹ I am a stranger in the earth: hide not thy commandments from me.

²⁰ My soul breaketh for the longing that it hath unto thy judgments at all times.

²¹ Thou hast rebuked the proud that are cursed, which do err from thy commandments.

Boldly Say: Father in the name of Jesus, I thank you that I do have this treasure in an earthly vessel that the excellent of the power may be of you and not of me. Father I thank you that the earth is the LORD and the fullness thereof, and I do belong to you, for you are my very own Father and I am your very own child. Father I thank you that your word is food to me.

Father I thank you for keeping me from proud. Father I thank you that you are my very own Father and I am your very own child. I am sheep of your pasture, I am bone of the bone of Jesus and flesh of the flesh of Jesus, what is true of him is true of me, for everything begat his kind. Father I thank you that as Jesus is so I am in this world, my desire is to relate to you as he related to you in his earthly walk. Father I pray that I will walk, talk, and relate to people as Jesus did in his earthly walk, Father I pray that I will always reach out to sinners with the gospel of Jesus Christ, in Jesus name, Amen.

²² Remove from me reproach and contempt; for I have kept thy testimonies.

²³ Princes also did sit and speak against me: but thy servant did meditate in thy statutes.

²⁴ Thy testimonies also are my delight and my counselors.

Boldly Say: Father in the name of Jesus, I thank you for removing from me reproach and contempt, for your word is my delight and my greatest treasure. Father I thank you that your word is sweeter than honey to my taste. Father I thank you that I am doer of your word. Oh God! The testimonies of your word are in me. There are those that rise against me, but my trust is thy word. Father I thank you that you are a shield about me. Father I thank you that your testimonies are my delight and my counselors. Father I thank you that your testimonies are true and sure, for your right hand has brought salvation to me, in Jesus name, Amen.

25 My soul cleaveth unto the dust: quicken thou me according to thy word.

26 I have declared my ways, and thou heardest me: teach me thy statutes.

27 Make me to understand the way of thy precepts: so shall I talk of thy wondrous works.

Boldly Say: Father in the name of Jesus, I thank you for quicken me according to your word. Father I thank you that your word is a lamp unto my feet and a light unto my path. Father I thank you that your word is like a hidden treasure to me, in which I have committed my all to discover. Father I thank you that your word have I hidden in my heart that I may not sin against thee. Father I exalt your word above everything, Father how amicable is your word, teach me your word. Father I acknowledge that understanding comes from you. Father I ask that you give me understanding of your word, that I may rightly divide your word and live by your word, that your name may be glorify in me and through me, in Jesus name, Amen.

²⁸ My soul melteth for heaviness: strengthen thou me according unto thy word.

²⁹ Remove from me the way of lying: and grant me thy law graciously.

³⁰ I have chosen the way of truth: thy judgments have I laid before me.

Boldly Say: Father in the name of Jesus, I thank you that you are for me. Father I thank you that you are my very own Father and I am your very own child. Father I pray that you will strengthen me with might by your Holy Spirit that dwells in me and according to your word. Father I thank you for removing from me the way of lying and grant me your word graciously. Father I thank you for your word said lie not one to another. Father I pray that I will always seek truth, for your word is truth. Father I thank you that your word is always before me, O how I love your word; it is my meditation all day, in Jesus name, Amen.

31 I have stuck unto thy testimonies: O LORD, put me not to shame.

32 I will run the way of thy commandments, when thou shalt enlarge my heart.

33 Teach me, O LORD, the way of thy statutes; and I shall keep it unto the end.

Boldly Say: Father in the name of Jesus, Father I thank you that your word is dwelling in me. Father I thank you that I do abide in you and your word do abide in me. Father I thank you that your word is my daily desirer. Father I thank you that I do run the way of your word. Father I thank you that your word is my mirror and I do daily put your word before me. Father I pray you will daily teach me your word; I will keep it unto the end, in Jesus name, Amen.

³⁴ Give me understanding, and I shall keep thy law; yea, I shall observe it with my whole heart.

³⁵ Make me to go in the path of thy commandments; for therein do I delight.

³⁶ Incline my heart unto thy testimonies, and not to covetousness.

Boldly Say: Father in the name of Jesus, I thank you that it is by grace I am saved through faith; and that not of myself: it is your gift. Father I pray that you will give me understanding and I will keep your word. Father I thank you that your grace in me is sufficient for me to act on your word. Father thank for leading me to go the path of your word; for therein do I delight. Father inclines my heart unto your word, and not to covetousness, in Jesus name, Amen.

[37] **Turn away mine eyes from beholding vanity; and quicken thou me in thy way.**

[38] **Stablish thy word unto thy servant, who is devoted to thy fear.**

[39] **Turn away my reproach which I fear: for thy judgments are good.**

Boldly Say: Father in the name of Jesus, I Pray that you will turn mine eyes from beholding vanity: and quicken me by your word. Father I thank you that I always put your word before me, Father I thank you that your word is a lamp unto feet and a light unto my path. Father I thank you that your word have I hid in my heart that I may not sin against thee. Father I pray you will stablish your word unto me, for I do delight in your word and I do reverence you. Father I pray you will turn away my reproach and manifest yourself through me, that the name of Jesus Christ may be glorify in me and through me, in Jesus name, Amen.

40 Behold, I have longed after thy precepts: quicken me in thy righteousness.

41 Let thy mercies come also unto me, O LORD, even thy salvation, according to thy word.

42 So shall I have wherewith to answer him that reproacheth me: for I trust in thy word.

Boldly Say: Father in the name of Jesus, I thank you for your word. Father I thank you that I daily hungry for your word, for your word is food to me. I do go after your word as person in a desert that has not eat or drink water for days. Father, it is your word only can satisfy the hungry and the taste. Father, salvation belongs to you;

your right hand has brought salvation to me. Now, I do have hope and readiness to answer anyone about the hope that is within me, in Jesus name, Amen.

43 **And take not the word of truth utterly out of my mouth; for I have hoped in thy judgments.**

44 **So shall I keep thy law continually for ever and ever.**

45 **And I will walk at liberty: for I seek thy precepts.**

Boldly Say: Father in the name of Jesus, I thank you for sanctifying me by thy truth, thou word is truth. Father I thank you that your word is forever in my mouth. Father I thank you that your word have I hid in my heart that I may not sin against thee. Father I thank you that I am a doer of your word. Father I thank you that your word is a lamp unto my feet and a light unto my path. Father I thank you that my hands are clean because I do take heed to your word. Father I thank you that I am cleanse by your word. Father I thank you that I do love your word and I do have great peace, and nothing shall offend me. Father I thank you that because of your word in me and your grace towards me, I do walk in the liberty whereby Jesus Christ has set me free, and I do not entangled again with the yoke of bondage, in Jesus name, Amen.

46 I will speak of thy testimonies also before kings, and will not be ashamed.

47 And I will delight myself in thy commandments, which I have loved.

48 My hands also will I lift up unto thy commandments, which I have loved; and I will meditate in thy statutes.

Boldly Say: Father in the name of Jesus, I thank you that I am not ashamed of the gospel of Jesus Christ, for it is your power unto salvation to everyone that believes. Father I thank you for revealing your great salvation through your Holy Spirit by the peaching of the gospel of Jesus Christ. Father I thank you that none is too little and none is too great to hear the gospel. As it is written: for God so love the world: that he gave his only begotten Son, that whosoever believe in him, should not perish but have everlasting life. Father I thank you that your word is my uttermost delight. Father in Jesus name, I totally surrender my spirit, soul, and body to you. Father I surrender my all to your word, in Jesus name, Amen.

⁴⁹ Remember the word unto thy servant, upon which thou hast caused me to hope.

⁵⁰ This is my comfort in my affliction: for thy word hath quickened me.

⁵¹ The proud have had me greatly in derision: yet have I not declined from thy law.

**Boldly Say:** Father in the name of Jesus, I thank you for your word. Father I thank you that your word is forever alive in me. Father I thank you for your Holy Spirit that dwells in me forever. Father I thank you for your Holy Spirit in me that does bring your word to my remembrance and does show me things to come; that is, he does show me the future. Father I thank you that in every situation your word tells me what to do, Father I thank you that you always fight for me. Therefore, I will always stand still and see your salvation for me, in Jesus name, Amen.

⁵² I remembered thy judgments of old, O LORD; and have comforted myself.

⁵³ Horror hath taken hold upon me because of the wicked that forsake thy law.

⁵⁴ Thy statutes have been my songs in the house of my pilgrimage.

Boldly Say: Father in the name of Jesus, I thank you for your word. Father I thank you for the comfort of your word to me. Father I thank you for the various triumphant you gave to me in the past when I acted on your word. Father I thank you for the comfort and peace your word gave to me in the time of trouble. Father I thank you for your word which quicken me to believe in hope against hope, for I know that my Redeemer lives and he will stand for me and with me against the evil one. Father I thank you that while I am in this tabernacle, I will continue to praise you, no matter how I feel because you are my very own Father and I am your very own child, in Jesus name, Amen.

⁵⁵ I have remembered thy name, O LORD, in the night, and have kept thy law.

⁵⁶ This I had, because I kept thy precepts.

⁵⁷ Thou art my portion, O LORD: I have said that I would keep thy words.

Boldly Say: Father in the name of Jesus, I thank you for your Holy Spirit and for your word. Father I thank you that without your Holy Spirit and your word I will not know you. Father I thank you for your Holy Spirit that always bring your word to my remembrance. Father I thank you for your word that continuously come to my mind in the depth of night when I woke up, which speak to me and refresh me. I am very grateful to you.

Father I thank you that I am a doer of your word. Father I thank you that you are my portion, in Jesus name, Amen.

⁵⁸ I intreated thy favour with my whole heart: be merciful unto me according to thy word.

⁵⁹ I thought on my ways, and turned my feet unto thy testimonies.

⁶⁰ I made haste, and delayed not to keep thy commandments.

Boldly Say: Father in the name of Jesus, I thank you for your word. Father I thank you that the entrance of your word giveth light. Father I thank you that your word is a light unto my feet and a lamp unto my path. Father I thank you for your favour. Father I thank you for given me favour with you and favour with people. Father I thank you that your favour does encamp around me. Father I thought on my ways and by your grace I determine to governor my ways with your word. Father I thank you that you hasten to perform your word in me and through me. Father I thank you that I hasten to repent, I hasten to forgive, I hasten to act on your word, in Jesus name, Amen.

⁶¹ The bands of the wicked have robbed me: but I have not forgotten thy law.

⁶² At midnight I will rise to give thanks unto thee because of thy righteous judgments.

⁶³ I am a companion of all them that fear thee, and of them that keep thy precepts.

Boldly Say: Father in the name of Jesus, I thank you for your word. Father I thank you for your Holy Spirit that guide and lead me to all truth. Father I thank you for the comfort that your Holy Spirit and your word gives to me in the midst of trouble. Father I thank you that you are always ever present in time of trouble. Father I thank you that at midnight I will arise to give thanks to you because of your precious word and your righteous judgments. Father I thank you that I do fellowship with people of like precious faith. Father I thank you that where two or three are gather together in the name of Jesus, you will be in the midst of them, in Jesus name, Amen.

64 The earth, O L ORD, is full of thy mercy: teach me thy statutes.

65 Thou hast dealt well with thy servant, O L ORD, according unto thy word.

66 Teach me good judgment and knowledge: for I have believed thy commandments.

Boldly Say: Father in the name of Jesus, I thank you for your word. Father I thank you that the earth is full of your mercy. Father I thank you that I do daily enjoy your mercy, Father I thank you that you surround me with your mercy. Father I pray that you will teach me your word daily through your Holy Spirit that dwell in me, for I am teachable and I am ever hungry for your precious word. Father I thank you that you have dealt with me according to your word that lives and abide forever. Father I pray that you will teach me good judgment and knowledge: for I have believed your precious word, in Jesus name, Amen.

⁶⁷ **Before I was afflicted I went astray: but now have I kept thy word.**

⁶⁸ **Thou art good, and doest good; teach me thy statutes.**

⁶⁹ **The proud have forged a lie against me: but I will keep thy precepts with my whole heart.**

Boldly Say: Father in the name of Jesus, I thank you for your unperishable word. Father I thank you that who you love you chastise and correct for the good of that individual. Father I thank you that you are faithful to correct me by your Holy Spirit and your precious word. Father I thank you that you are a loving Father and a good Father. Father I love you and I thank you that you always work everything for my good. Father I pray that I will always wholly put my trust in you and in your unconditional love for me. Father I thank that though the wicked my surround me, my trust is in you, for you said they shall surely gather together but not by you, and whosoever shall gather together against me shall fall for my sake. Father I thank you that you that is in me, is greater that the evil one and his cohorts that is in the world, in Jesus name, Amen.

70 Their heart is as fat as grease; but I delight in thy law.

71 It is good for me that I have been afflicted; that I might learn thy statutes.

72 The law of thy mouth is better unto me than thousands of gold and silver.

Boldly Say: Father in the name of Jesus, I thank you for your word. Father I thank you that sins, sickness, diseases, pains, problems, and troubles does not come from you, but comes from the evil one and through those the evil one expresses himself through, nevertheless, Father you are a loving Father and you are the solution and the answer to those evil things. Father I thank you that my spirit, soul, and body belongs to you, Father I thank you that the evil one has nothing in me. Father I thank you that whenever the evil one come against me, it is an opportunity for me to act on your word concern the situation, so that the name of Christ will be glorify. Father I thank you that I do delight in your word and your word is better than riches, in Jesus name, Amen.

⁷³ Thy hands have made me and fashioned me: give me understanding, that I may learn thy commandments.

⁷⁴ They that fear thee will be glad when they see me; because I have hoped in thy word.

⁷⁵ I know, O LORD, that thy judgments are right, and that thou in faithfulness hast afflicted me.

Boldly Say: Father in the name of Jesus, I thank you for your word. Father I thank you that you gave birth to me by your word through your Holy Spirit. Father I thank you that I am fearfully and wonderfully made by you. Father I thank you that your hands have made me and fashioned me: give me understanding, that I may learn thy word. Father I thank you that they that love you will be glad to see me because they shall see you in me, and they will know that I do represent Jesus Christ here on earth, while Jesus Christ present me in the heavens. Father I know your word is truth, Father I thank you that every good gifts come from you and every evil things come from the devil. Father I thank you that I can say boldly you are my very own Father and I am your very own child, in Jesus name, Amen.

⁷⁶ Let, I pray thee, thy merciful kindness be for my comfort, according to thy word unto thy servant.

⁷⁷ Let thy tender mercies come unto me, that I may live: for thy law is my delight.

⁷⁸ Let the proud be ashamed; for they dealt perversely with me without a cause: but I will meditate in thy precepts.

Boldly Say: Father in the name of Jesus, I thank you for your precious word. Father I thank you for your merciful kindness toward me according to your word. Father I pray that I will always acknowledge your tender mercies towards me and around

me, for I do delight in your word.
Father I thank you that your word is a
lamp unto my feet and a light unto my
path. Father I thank you that no
weapon that is form against me shall
prosper and I condemn every tongue
that rises against me in judgment, for
this is my heritage in the Lord and my
righteousness is of the LORD. Father I
thank you that your word is the
meditation of my heart all day, in Jesus
name, Amen.

⁷⁹ Let those that fear thee turn unto me, and those that have known thy testimonies.

⁸⁰ Let my heart be sound in thy statutes; that I be not ashamed.

⁸¹ My soul fainteth for thy salvation: but I hope in thy word.

<u>Boldly Say:</u> Father in the name of Jesus, I thank you for your ever living word. Father I thank you that I do love you. Father I thank you for our relationship. Father I thank you that you are always present with me and we can talk to each other without any interference. Father I thank you that I can talk to you about anything that concern me and you are always present to listen, and not only do you listen to me but you also respond to me. Father I thank you that you can speak to me at any time and in anywhere, I will listen and I will respond. Father I thank you that those that love, reverence and know you, and also know your word will receive me because I came from you. Father I pray that I will always rightly divide your word and make righteous judgment with mercy. Father I thank you for your salvation which is sure and forever settled, in Jesus name, Amen.

[82] Mine eyes fail for thy word, saying, When wilt thou comfort me?

[83] For I am become like a bottle in the smoke; yet do I not forget thy statutes.

[84] How many are the days of thy servant? when wilt thou execute judgment on them that persecute me?

Boldly Say: Father in the name of Jesus, I thank you that forever O Lord your word is settled in heaven. Father I pray that I will not be discourage about whatever is happening around me, for I know my Redeemer lives and he is for me and forever with me. Father I thank you that your word always comfort me, when I face opposing forces, trials and tribulations. Father I thank you and I pray that I will never forget your word in times of trials and tribulations. Father I thank you that I am always steadfast and unmovable, abiding in your word. Father I thank you that I am not worry of any situation for you told me to cast all my cares upon you for you care for me. Father I judge your word faithful. Therefore, Father I cast all my cares upon, for you care for me. Father I thank you that you are a loving Father and you always take care of me affectionately, in Jesus name, Amen.

85 The proud have digged pits for me, which are not after thy law.

86 All thy commandments are faithful: they persecute me wrongfully; help thou me.

87 They had almost consumed me upon earth; but I forsook not thy precepts.

Boldly Say: Father in the name of Jesus, I thank you for your word. Father I thank you that the disciple is not above his master. Father I thank you that if they persecuted Jesus Christ they will persecuted any true Christian that refuse to compromise, Father I pray that I will never compromise in the midst of persecution. Father I thank you that your word is truth. Father I thank you that your word is faithful and just, Father I thank you that you do always watch over your word to perform it. Father I thank you that I am true to you for you are my very own Father and I am your very own child. Father I thank you that your word is life to me, in Jesus name, Amen.

⁸⁸ Quicken me after thy lovingkindness; so shall I keep the testimony of thy mouth.

⁸⁹ For ever, O L<small>ORD</small>, thy word is settled in heaven.

⁹⁰ Thy faithfulness is unto all generations: thou hast established the earth, and it abideth.

Boldly Say: Father in the name of Jesus, I thank you for your word, Father I thank you for your word that quicken me daily. Father I thank you that your word to me is greater than all riches. Father I pray that you will give me continuous hunger for your word, yes Lord, hunger that nothing else can satisfy but your word only can satisfy. Father I thank you that For ever, O

LORD, thy word is settled in heaven. Father I thank you that your word does not need any improvement, let every man be a liar but God remain faithful. Father I thank you that I can rest on your word for it is forever settled in heaven. Father I thank you that your faithfulness is unto all generation; the earth is yours and the fullness thereof, for you have established the earth, and it remain, in Jesus name, Amen.

91 They continue this day according to thine ordinances: for all are thy servants.

92 Unless thy law had been my delights, I should then have perished in mine affliction.

93 I will never forget thy precepts: for with them thou hast quickened me.

Boldly Say: Father in the name of Jesus, I thank you for your word. Father I thank you that the earth is yours and all that are therein, for they continue according to your ordinances and you are my very own Father and I am your very own child. Father I thank you that you uphold all things by the word of your power. Father I thank you for teaching me the word of your power. Father I thank you for your word that always encourage me in time of trouble. Father I thank you that I will never forget your word because your word is life to me, in Jesus name, Amen.

94 I am thine, save me: for I have sought thy precepts.

95 The wicked have waited for me to destroy me: but I will consider thy testimonies.

96 I have seen an end of all perfection: but thy commandment is exceeding broad.

Boldly Say: Father in the name of Jesus, I thank you for your word. Father I thank you that you are my very own Father and I am your very own child. Father I thank you that whosoever plan evil against me touch the apple of your eyes. Father I thank you that whosoever dig a pit for me shall fall into the pit. Father I thank you that they shall gather together but not by you, whosoever shall gather together against me shall fall for my sake. Father I thank you that no matter what confront me, my trust is in you and in your word, not in the problem. Father I thank you that you do always expose my enemies to me. Father I thank you that you that is in me is great than the evil one that is in the world. Father I boldly confess to all the spiritual world and dimension; that I am more than conquerors through Jesus Christ who love me and gave himself for me, in Jesus name, Amen.

⁹⁷ O how love I thy law! it is my meditation all the day.

⁹⁸ Thou through thy commandments hast made me wiser than mine enemies: for they are ever with me.

⁹⁹ I have more understanding than all my teachers: for thy testimonies are my meditation.

Boldly Say: Father in the name of Jesus, I thank you for your word. Father I thank you that your word is lamp unto my feet and a light unto my path. O how I love your word! Your word is my mediation all the day. Father I thank you that your word is sweeter that honey to my taste. Father I thank you that your word is greater than many riches. Father I thank you that you have made Christ Jesus unto me wisdom. Father I thank you that your word does abide in me and I do abide in your word. Father I thank you that because you made Christ Jesus unto me wisdom and Christ in me the hope of glory: I am wiser than my enemies. Father I thank you that I do have more understanding than all my teachers, for your word is my meditation, in Jesus name, Amen.

100 I understand more than the ancients, because I keep thy precepts.

101 I have refrained my feet from every evil way, that I might keep thy word.

102 I have not departed from thy judgments: for thou hast taught me.

Boldly Say: Father in the name of Jesus, I thank you for your word. Father I thank you that I do have the mind of Christ. Father I thank you that your word is dwelling in me mightily. Father I thank you that I understand more than the ancient, because I love your word and I am a doer of your word. Father I thank you that I do put your word above people and things. Father I thank you for the privilege to live by your word, for man shall not live by bread alone but every word that proceeded out of your mouth. Father I thank you that I do refrain my feet from every evil way, for I am a doer of your word. Father I thank you that I have hidden your word in my heart. Father I thank you that I do provide things honest in the sight of all men. Father I thank you that I am abiding in your word forever and your word does abiding in me forever, in Jesus name, Amen.

103 How sweet are thy words unto my taste! yea, sweeter than honey to my mouth!

104 Through thy precepts I get understanding: therefore I hate every false way.

105 Thy word is a lamp unto my feet, and a light unto my path.

Boldly Say: Father in the name of Jesus, I thank you for your precious word. Father I thank you that there is no problem, situation and condition in this present world that your word does not have answer for or solution, Father I thank you that you have given unto me all things pertaining unto life and godliness. O how sweet are your words unto my taste! Yea, sweeter than honey to my mouth. Father I thank you that I do enjoy reading, meditating and doing your word daily. Father I thank you that the entrance of your word does give me light. Father I thank you that through your words and your grace I do have understanding: therefore do I hate every false way and that which is evil. Father I thank you that your word is a lamp unto my feet, and light unto my path. Father I thank you that your word does give me direction in life, in Jesus name, Amen.

106 I have sworn, and I will perform it, that I will keep thy righteous judgments.

107 I am afflicted very much: quicken me, O LORD, according unto thy word.

108 Accept, I beseech thee, the freewill offerings of my mouth, O LORD, and teach me thy judgments.

Boldly Say: Father in the name of Jesus, I thank you for your ever living word. Father I thank you that except you build the house, they that labour, labour in vain. Father I thank you that your word is ever before me, Father I thank you that I have set my heart on your word and I have settled it in my heart to perform your word regardless how I feel, for the just shall live by faith. Father I thank you that I do walk by faith and not by sight. Father I thank you that while I look not to the things I see but to the things I do not see, for the things which I do see are temporary but the things which I do not see are eternal. Father I thank you that in time of problem and trouble, you do always quicken me according to your word. Father I thank you that in time of problem and trouble, I do call on you and you do answer me and you do faithfully delivered me. Father I thank you that unto you do I offer continuously the sacrifice of praise which is the fruit my lips, in Jesus name, Amen.

109 My soul is continually in my hand: yet do I not forget thy law.

110 The wicked have laid a snare for me: yet I erred not from thy precepts.

111 Thy testimonies have I taken as an heritage for ever: for they are the rejoicing of my heart.

Boldly Say: Father in the name of Jesus, I thank you for your word. Father I thank you that your word is a lamp unto my feet and a light unto my path. Father I thank you for your word said choose you these day who you will serve, Father I thank you that I forever cast my lot on you to serve you all the days of life. Father I thank you that you alone is my portion. Father I thank you that I am in the world but I am not of the world. Father I thank you that the world is crucified unto me and I am crucified unto the world. Father I thank you that I do obey you more than people. Father I thank you that I do not live to please the world but I live to please you. Father I thank you that to obey is better than sacrifices. Father I thank you that I do boldly act on your word in this crocked and perverted world. Father I thank you that your word have I taken as an heritage for ever: for they are the rejoicing of my heart. Father I thank you for your word does cause me to rejoice as one that has found great riches, in Jesus name, Amen.

112 I have inclined mine heart to perform thy statutes alway, even unto the end.

113 I hate vain thoughts: but thy law do I love.

114 Thou art my hiding place and my shield: I hope in thy word.

Boldly Say: Father in the name of Jesus, I thank you for your word. Father I have inclined mine heart to perform your word always, even unto the end. Father I thank you that partial obey is disobedient. Father I thank you that I do wholly follow you my LORD and GOD. Father I thank you for your Holy Spirit that dwells in me forever, which guide me and lead me to all truth. Father I thank you that I do hate vain thoughts: but your word do I love.

Father I thank you that I only think on whatsoever things are true, whatsoever things are honest, whatsoever things are just, whatsoever things are pure, whatsoever things are lovely, whatsoever things are of good report; if there be any virtue, and if there be any praise. Father I thank you that you are my hiding place and my shield: I hope in your word. Father I thank you that you are my High Tower. Father I thank you that in you I live, move and have my being, in Jesus name, Amen.

[115] Depart from me, ye evildoers: for I will keep the commandments of my God.

[116] Uphold me according unto thy word, that I may live: and let me not be ashamed of my hope.

[117] Hold thou me up, and I shall be safe: and I will have respect unto thy statutes continually.

Boldly Say: Father in the name of Jesus, I thank you for your word. Father I thank you that your word said I should not be unequally yoke together with unbelievers, for fellowship does light have with darkness. Father I thank you that I do provide things honest in the sight of all men. Father I thank you that I am a doer of your word. Father upholds me according unto your word, that I may live: and let me not be ashamed of my hope. Father I thank you that my hope is in you and in your word. Father I thank you for holding me up above my enemies and things, that your word may be magnify in me and through me, that the mane of Jesus Christ may be glorify in all I do and say. Father I thank you that it is Christ in all and all, in Jesus name, Amen.

¹¹⁸ Thou hast trodden down all them that err from thy statutes: for their deceit is falsehood.

¹¹⁹ Thou puttest away all the wicked of the earth like dross: therefore I love thy testimonies.

¹²⁰ My flesh trembleth for fear of thee; and I am afraid of thy judgments.

Boldly Say: Father in the name of Jesus, I thank you for your word. Father I thank you that the entrance of your word gives light. Father I thank you that your word said "be not deceive God is not mocked, whatsoever a man soweth that shall he also reap." Father I thank you that your word said "While the earth remaineth, seedtime and harvest, and cold and heat, and summer and winter, and day and night shall not cease." Father I thank you that the Sower went to sow a seed, and that seed is your word. Father I thank you that you do teach me to sow your word into my life with my mouth continuously. Father I thank you that I am not weary in well doing and I am not discourage because I know that in due time I shall reap great harvest. Father I thank you that I do reverence your word. Father I thank you that at your appointed time the wicked shall be cut off, in Jesus name, Amen.

121 I have done judgment and justice: leave me not to mine oppressors.

122 Be surety for thy servant for good: let not the proud oppress me.

123 Mine eyes fail for thy salvation, and for the word of thy righteousness.

Boldly Say: Father in the name of Jesus, I thank you for your word. Father I thank you that I do esteem your word above my necessary food. Father I thank you that I do delight myself in your word. Father I thank you that your word is sweeter than honey to my taste. Father I thank you that I am a doer of your word, Father I thank you that you said you will never leave me nor forsake me, that I may boldly say the Lord is my helper what can man do unto me. Father I thank you that I do believe in you and in your word. Father I thank you that your covenant with me is sure, and Jesus Christ is the Surety of the covenant. Father I thank you that I am your righteousness in Christ Jesus, in Jesus name, Amen.

¹²⁴ **Deal with thy servant according unto thy mercy, and teach me thy statutes.**

¹²⁵ **I am thy servant; give me understanding, that I may know thy testimonies.**

¹²⁶ **It is time for thee, LORD, to work: for they have made void thy law.**

<u>Boldly Say:</u> Father in the name of Jesus, I thank you for your word. Father I thank you that your mercy endurance forever. Father I thank you that your mercy toward me is forever and they are new every day. Father I thank you also for your faithfulness towards me daily for they are great. Father I ask that you teach me your word daily. Father I pray that you grant me understanding of your word that I may do it. Father I thank you that you always manifest your word through believers and unbelievers because you love people, in Jesus name, Amen.

¹²⁷ Therefore I love thy commandments above gold; yea, above fine gold.

¹²⁸ Therefore I esteem all thy precepts concerning all things to be right; and I hate every false way.

¹²⁹ Thy testimonies are wonderful: therefore doth my soul keep them.

Boldly Say: Father in the name of Jesus, I thank you for your word. Father I thank you that your word is more precious than gold. Father I thank you that your word is sweeter than honey to my taste. Father I thank you that your word is mightier than any earthly weapon. Father I thank you that your word is life. Father I thank you that your word is the only thing that clean the dirtiest life on earth. Father I thank you that your word is truth. Let every man be a liar but God remain truth. Father I thank you that I do love what you love and I do hate what you hate. Father I thank you that your words are wonderful and does brings joy to my soul, in Jesus name, Amen.

130 The entrance of thy words giveth light; it giveth understanding unto the simple.

131 I opened my mouth, and panted: for I longed for thy commandments.

132 Look thou upon me, and be merciful unto me, as thou usest to do unto those that love thy name.

Boldly Say: Father in the name of Jesus, I thank you for your word. Father I thank you that the entrance of your word into my life does give me light, it gives me understanding on how to governor my life and my lifestyle. Father I thank you that I am always longing for your word, longing to spend time with you alone. Father I thank you that in your presence is fullness of joy, at your right is pleasure forever. Father I thank you that you said in your word you will never leave me nor forsake me, that you will be with me forever, Father I believe your word. Father you said you will help me. Father I rest on your word, in Jesus name, Amen.

¹³³ Order my steps in thy word: and let not any iniquity have dominion over me.

¹³⁴ Deliver me from the oppression of man: so will I keep thy precepts.

¹³⁵ Make thy face to shine upon thy servant; and teach me thy statutes.

Boldly Say: Father in the name of Jesus, I thank you for your word. Father I pray that you will order my steps in your word. Father I pray that I will not let sin have dominion over me, for in Christ Jesus I live, move, and have my being. Father I thank you that you have delivered me from the power of darkness and translated me into the kingdom of your dear Son Christ

Jesus, in whom I have my redemption through the precious blood of Jesus Christ. Father I thank you for delivering me from the power of darkness into the kingdom of light. Father I thank you for making your face to shine upon me for you are my very own Father and I am your very own child. Father I ask that you will teach me your word and I will do it, in Jesus name, Amen.

¹³⁶ Rivers of waters run down mine eyes, because they keep not thy law.

¹³⁷ Righteous art thou, O LORD, and upright are thy judgments.

¹³⁸ Thy testimonies that thou hast commanded are righteous and very faithful.

Boldly Say: Father in the name of Jesus, I thank you for your word. Father I thank you that except you build the house they that labour, labour in vain. Father I thank you that your word is not bound. Father I thank that you are always looking for someone to stand in the gap for soul and intercede, Father I am available to stand in the gap and intercede for the salvation of soul, yes Lord, for souls to come and receive the salvation that Jesus Christ purchase for them. Father I thank you that you are righteous and you are upright in your judgment. Father I thank you that it is not your will for any soul to perish but that all should come to repentance. Father I thank you that you have no pleasure in the death of the wicked. Father I thank you that you so love this world, yes people, that you gave your begotten Son that whosoever believe in him should not perish but have everlasting life. Father I thank you that you did not send your Son into the world to condemn the world but you send him to save people from your wrath which is to come. Father I am available for your grace to enable me to look for an opportunity or create an opportunity to share Jesus Christ with someone daily. Father I thank you that your words are righteous and faithful, in Jesus name, Amen.

139 My zeal hath consumed me, because mine enemies have forgotten thy words.

140 Thy word is very pure: therefore thy servant loveth it.

141 I am small and despised: yet do not I forget thy precepts.

Boldly Say: Father in the name of Jesus, I thank you for your word, Father I thank you that your word has consumed me for I always hungry for your word. Father I thank you that your word have I hid in my heart that I might not sin against thee. Father I thank you that your word is light to me in the midst of a dark world. Father I thank you that you said I am light in this world, Father I believe your word.

Father I thank you that your word is pure; therefore, I do love your word. Father I thank you that I am in the world but I am not of the world. Father I thank you that the world is crucified unto me and I am crucified unto the world. Father I thank you that I only seek the praises that come from you, in Jesus name, Amen.

[142] Thy righteousness is an everlasting righteousness, and thy law is the truth.

[143] Trouble and anguish have taken hold on me: yet thy commandments are my delights.

[144] The righteousness of thy testimonies is everlasting: give me understanding, and I shall live.

Boldly Say: Father in the name of Jesus, I thank you for your word. Father I thank you that your righteousness is an everlasting righteousness and your word is truth. Father I thank you for you have made Christ Jesus unto me righteousness. Father I thank you for sanctifying me by the truth, your word is truth. Father

I thank you that you said you will be with me in trouble, Father I do believe you. Father I thank you that your word is my delight. Father I thank you that you are righteous and your word is everlasting. Father I thank you for you have made Christ Jesus unto me wisdom. Father I thank you that I do have the mind of Christ. Father I thank you that with long life will you satisfy me and show me your salvation, in Jesus name, Amen.

¹⁴⁵ I cried with my whole heart; hear me, O LORD: I will keep thy statutes.

¹⁴⁶ I cried unto thee; save me, and I shall keep thy testimonies.

¹⁴⁷ I prevented the dawning of the morning, and cried: I hoped in thy word.

Boldly Say: Father in the name of Jesus, I thank you for your word. Father I thank you that I am forever hungry for your precious word. Father I thank you that your word is a lamp unto my feet and a light unto my path. Father I thank you that I am a doer of your word. Father I thank you that Christ in me is the hope of glory. Father I thank you that I am never alone, for you said you will never leave me nor forsake me, so that I can boldly say the Lord is my helper, and I will not fear what man shall do unto me. Father I thank you for inviting me to come boldly unto the throne of grace, that I may obtain mercy, and find grace to help in time of need, in Jesus name, Amen.

148 Mine eyes prevent the night watches, that I might meditate in thy word.

149 Hear my voice according unto thy lovingkindness: O LORD, quicken me according to thy judgment.

150 They draw nigh that follow after mischief: they are far from thy law.

Boldly Say: Father in the name of Jesus, I thank you for your word. Father I thank you that your word is the meditation of my heart. Father I thank you that your word have I hid in my heart that I might not sin against thee. Father I thank you that I am dominant and consumed by your precious word. Father I thank you that I am cleanse by your word. Father I thank you that the entrance of your word gives light. Father I thank you that your words does produce life in me, therefore, I love your word. Father I thank you that I am not worry about evil doers because their days are short. Father I thank you for you will repay evil doers for their evil deeds. Father I thank you that is always darkness before the evil doers. Father I thank you that the righteous shall shine as the noon day sun, in Jesus name, Amen.

151 Thou art near, O LORD; and all thy commandments are truth.

152 Concerning thy testimonies, I have known of old that thou hast founded them for ever.

153 Consider mine affliction, and deliver me: for I do not forget thy law.

Boldly Say: Father in the name of Jesus, I thank you for your word. Father I thank you for you said you will never leave me nor forsake me, Father I believe you and your word. Father I thank you for you said Lo I am with you, Father I believe you and your word. Father I thank you that your word is truth. Father I thank you that your word is forever settled in heaven. Father I thank you that I forever settled it in my heart to live by your word, for your word is life. Father I thank you that I do not forget your word. Father I thank you that in time of trouble, I called on you and you answered me and delivered me from all my troubles, therefore, I rejoice and praise your holy name, in Jesus name, Amen.

154 Plead my cause, and deliver me: quicken me according to thy word.

155 Salvation is far from the wicked: for they seek not thy statutes.

156 Great are thy tender mercies, O LORD: quicken me according to thy judgments.

Boldly Say: Father in the name of Jesus, I thank you for your word. Father I thank you for Jesus Christ and the great price he paid for my sin. Father I thank you for the blood of Jesus Christ that speaks of better things than that of Abel. Father I thank you for inviting me to come boldly to the throne of grace, that I may obtain mercy, and grace to help in time of

need, because of the finished work of
Jesus Christ. Father I pray the wicked
will come to accept the salvation Jesus
Christ is offering them, for you have
no pleasure in the death of the wicked.
Father I thank you for your mercies,
for great are your tender mercies
towards me. Father I thank you that
your mercies is always on me, around
me, and before me daily. Father I
thank you that your word does give me
life daily, in Jesus name, Amen.

¹⁵⁷ **Many are my persecutors and mine enemies; yet do I not decline from thy testimonies.**

¹⁵⁸ **I beheld the transgressors, and was grieved; because they kept not thy word.**

¹⁵⁹ **Consider how I love thy precepts: quicken me, O LORD, according to thy lovingkindness.**

Boldly Say: Father in the name of Jesus, I thank you for your word. Father I thank you for your word said they shall surely gather together, but not by you: whosoever shall gather together against me shall fall for my sake. Father I believe your word and I take your word to heart. Father I thank you that no weapon that is formed against me shall prosper and every tongue that shall rise against me in judgment, I do condemn, in Jesus name. Father I thank you for the grace to intercede for sinners to come to the salvation which Jesus Christ purchased for each of them. Father I thank you that I love your word, for it is the meditation of my heart all day, in Jesus name, Amen.

¹⁶⁰ Thy word is true from the beginning: and every one of thy righteous judgments endureth for ever.

¹⁶¹ Princes have persecuted me without a cause: but my heart standeth in awe of thy word.

¹⁶² I rejoice at thy word, as one that findeth great spoil.

<u>Boldly Say:</u> Father in the name of Jesus, I thank you for your word. Father I thank you that your word is true from the beginning; and every one of your righteous judgments endure forever. Father I thank you that forever O Lord your word is settled in heaven. Father I thank you that no weapon that is formed against me shall prosper and every tongue that shall rise against me in judgment, I do condemn. Father I thank you that Christ in me is greater than the evil one and all his cohorts that is in the world. Father I thank you that I do rejoice in your word as one that find great spoil, in Jesus name, Amen.

163 I hate and abhor lying: but thy law do I love.

164 Seven times a day do I praise thee because of thy righteous judgments.

165 Great peace have they which love thy law: and nothing shall offend them.

Boldly Say: Father in the name of Jesus, I thank you for your word. Father I thank you for your word said we that are born again should not lie one to another. Father I thank you that your word said we should speak the truth in love. Father I thank you that I have already put away lies and I do speak the truth in love. Father I thank you that the world is crucified unto me, and I am crucified unto the world. Father I thank you that I do praise you always and daily for who you are, for Jesus Christ, for your Holy Spirit who dwells in me, for your precious word, and for all your goodness towards me, my family, friends and people that I do not know. Father I thank you that great peace have they that love your word: and nothing shall offend them. Father I thank you that I do have great peace because I do your love your word: and nothing shall offend me, in Jesus name, Amen.

¹⁶⁶ LORD, I have hoped for thy salvation, and done thy commandments.

¹⁶⁷ My soul hath kept thy testimonies; and I love them exceedingly.

¹⁶⁸ I have kept thy precepts and thy testimonies: for all my ways are before thee.

Boldly Say: Father in the name of Jesus, I thank you for your word. Father I thank you that I am a doer of your word. Father I thank you for Jesus Christ who paid the uttermost price for my salvation and the salvation of everyone in the world. Father I am grateful for my salvation, for I can boldly call you my Father because I have accepted Jesus Christ as my Saviour and Lord. Father I thank you because I am your child I do keep your word, for I do love your word greatly and it is the meditation of my heart all day. Father I thank you that I do live by your word for my ways are open to your sight, in Jesus name, Amen.

169 Let my cry come near before thee, O LORD: give me understanding according to thy word.

170 Let my supplication come before thee: deliver me according to thy word.

171 My lips shall utter praise, when thou hast taught me thy statutes.

Boldly Say: Father in the name of Jesus, I thank you for your word. Father I greatly love your word. Father I pray you teach me your word and give me understanding according to your word that I may keep it. Father I thank you that you are my shield and bucker, you are my high tower, to you do I run to in time of trouble. Father I thank you that you always deliver me in trouble. Father you said I should call on you in the day of trouble and you will deliver me. Father you said you will never leave me nor forsake me. Father I believe you and your word. Father I thank you that you said you will help me. Father I take you at your word. Father I thank you and I praise you for daily teaching me your word, in Jesus name, Amen.

¹⁷² **My tongue shall speak of thy word: for all thy commandments are righteousness.**

¹⁷³ **Let thine hand help me; for I have chosen thy precepts.**

¹⁷⁴ **I have longed for thy salvation, O LORD; and thy law is my delight.**

Boldly Say: Father in the name of Jesus, I thank you for your word. My tongue shall speak of your word: for all your words are righteousness. Father I thank you that I do love to read your word, pray your word and sing your word. Father I thank you that your word is pure, your word is just, and your word is faithful. Father I thank you for you said in your precious word that you will help me. Father I thank you that except you build the house, they labour in vain that build it: except you keep the city, the watchman will stay up all night but in vain. Father I thank you that your right hand has brought salvation to me. Father I thank you that I do love your word and I can rest on your word, for your word is my delight, in Jesus name, Amen.

¹⁷⁵ Let my soul live, and it shall praise thee; and let thy judgments help me.

¹⁷⁶ I have gone astray like a lost sheep; seek thy servant; for I do not forget thy commandments.

Boldly Say: Father in the name of Jesus, I thank you for your precious, wonderful and sweet word. Father I thank you that your word is sweeter than honey to my taste. Father I thank you that your word is as a great spoil. Father I thank you that your word have I hid in my heart that I may not sin against you. Father I thank you that your word is pure. Father I thank you that with long life will you satisfy me and show me your salvation. Father I thank you that I shall praise you daily. Father I pray that I will never go astray form your precious word. Father I pray that you keep me as the apple of your eyes. Father I thank you and I pray that you will keep me from sin for I do belong to you. Father I thank you that you are my very own Father, and I am your very own child, in Jesus name, Amen.

SOIL Foundation, Inc.

All Books can be Purchase from amazon.com, Amazon.co.uk, Amazon.de, Amazon.fr, Amazon.it, Amazon.es, Barnesandnoble.com, ebay.com, (search: Ovbije Book)

Publication Books

All Day God

Praying the Word From the Book of Timothy

Praying the Word From the Book of Ephesians

Resurrection from the Flood

Coaching to Completion

Praying the Word From the Epistle of John

God Loves Me

God Is With Me
I Am Not Afraid

Praying the Word From the Book of
Galatians

Praying the Word From the Book of
James

Praying the Word From the Book of
Philippians

To God Alone
Praise, Worship & Thanksgivings

Praying the Word From the Book of
Colossians

Praying the Word From the Book of
Titus

Praying the Word From First Peter

Praying the Word Form Psalms 119

Libros en Español

Orando la Palabra
Desde el Libro de Efesios

Dios Me Ama

Tracts:

5 Things God wants you to know

Love Yourself

SONG

<u>JESUS WILL NEVER TURN YOU DOWN</u>

Jesus is a friend that will never turn you down

He will never leave you nor forsake you

Call on his name for he is there for you

He will save and guide you to the end

He will save and guide you

REPEAT

By

L. O. Ovbije

www.ingramcontent.com/pod-product-compliance
Lightning Source LLC
Chambersburg PA
CBHW061739020426
42331CB00006B/1298